Aberdeenshire Library and Information Service
www.aberdeenshire.gov.uk/libraries
Renewals Hotline 01224 661511

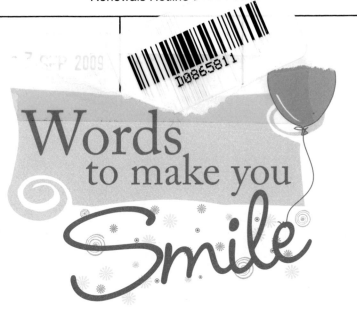

- 7 SEP 2009

D0865811

Words
to make you
Smile

ALIS
2663608

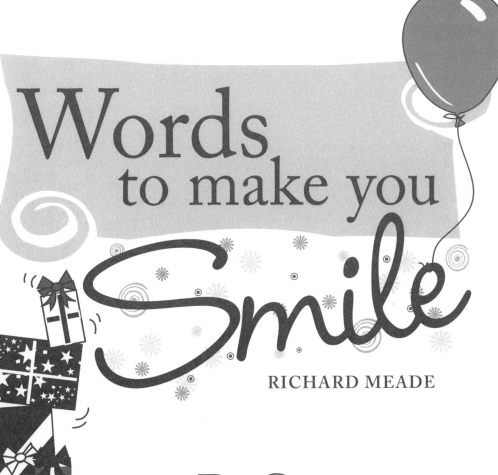

Words
to make you
Smile

RICHARD MEADE

D&C
David and Charles

A DAVID & CHARLES BOOK
Copyright © David & Charles Limited 2008

David & Charles is an F+W Media Inc. company
4700 East Galbraith Road
Cincinnati, OH 45236

Text copyright © Richard Meade 2008
Layout and Illustrations copyright © David & Charles
2008

Richard Meade has asserted his right to be identified
as author of this work in accordance with the
Copyright, Designs and Patents Act, 1988.

All rights reserved. No part of this publication may
be reproduced, stored in a retrieval system, or
transmitted, in any form or by any means, electronic
or mechanical, by photocopying, recording or
otherwise, without prior permission in writing from
the publisher.

A catalogue record for this book is available from the
British Library.

ISBN-13: 978-0-7153-3205-4 hardback
ISBN-10: 0-7153-3205-8 hardback

ISBN-13: 978-0-7153-3206-1 paperback
ISBN-10: 0-7153-3206-6 paperback

Printed in China by Shenzhen Donnelley Co Ltd
for David & Charles
Brunel House   Newton Abbot   Devon

Commissioning Editor Jane Trollope
Editorial Manager Emily Pitcher
Editorial Assistant James Brooks
Designer Sabine Eulau
Illustrator Mia Farrant
Production Controller Kelly Smith

Visit our website at www.davidandcharles.co.uk

David & Charles books are available from all
good bookshops; alternatively you can contact
our Orderline on 0870 9908222 or write to
us at FREEPOST EX2 110, D&C Direct, Newton
Abbot, TQ12 4ZZ (no stamp required UK only); US
customers call 800-289-0963 and Canadian
customers call 800-840-5220.

ABERDEENSHIRE LIBRARY AND	
INFORMATION SERVICES	
2663608	
HJ	2495275
821.92	£9.99
AD	ANF

Contents

6   ACKNOWLEDGMENTS
7   INTRODUCTION

8   Birthday Celebrations

32   Love is in the Air

62   Friends & Family

86   All Change

108   Party, Party, Party

138   Seasonal Greetings

180   Cheer Up

188   SUPPLIERS
191   ABOUT THE AUTHOR
192   INDEX

Acknowledgments

This book has my name on it but it's a product of all those who have been supportive of my scribbling over the years. It's dedicated to my parents Jan and Dave, my new wife Jenny, my cousin Simon, and to my Nan Ivy who would have been very happy for me.

I want to thank all the friends, family and other characters that have either been helpful or a source of inspiration! Thank you also to everyone at David & Charles and thanks to Sarah Crosland for helping to make this possible.

6

Intro

A collection of playful poems, witty one-liners and riotous rhymes to ensure your card is received with a smile. This book is written for those who specialise in crafting and want to add a comical touch to their makes.

Inside you'll find rhymes to make you giggle, chuckle and laugh-out-loud covering every occasion with each verse designed to give your card that finishing touch.

Whether it be a birthday, Christmas, new home or anniversary there's a clever concoction inside that's sure to go down a treat.

Birthday Celebrations

You're super old now, that's no lie,
And your life's been long and rich;
In fact when God said 'let there be light'
It was you that flicked the switch

There are no candles on your cake this year
It's for the best I'm afraid,
For the smoke from all those candles
Would surely attract the fire brigade

On your birthday you should do whatever you want... after all, old people can get away with anything!

We wanted to give you
the birthday bumps
But we've been told
we have to be cautious
Because now you've reached
such a ripe old age
We think they'd leave you
nauseous

Happy birthday! Let's raise a glass
And toast to your good health
We didn't know what to buy you,
So here's some cash to get it yourself

When we asked you to blow out the candles
on your birthday cake
We didn't realise that we were making
A terrible mistake
The sheer amount of candles
Had you huffing and puffing away
And by the time you had finished
It was no longer your birthday

You've lost all your looks and your beauty
Time's taken your swagger and grace
It's almost as hard to count up to your age
as it is to count the lines on your face

Now you've reached a difficult age where
you start to look back on your youth
You'll soon be buying motorbikes, wearing
leather and acting uncouth

As it's your birthday
I thought we could
have a quiet night in...
so we could save all
our money for my
birthday celebrations

Tip
40 can be
replaced with
a number of
other ages

You're always out on the go, or chatting with the girls
There's just no stopping you, you're out to rock the world
But now that you're 40 isn't it time you turned a page?
Surely you should buy a walking stick and start to act your age!

It's all right you acting 21
And partying the night away
But the fact is that you're 30
And you're starting to go grey
You can't be so outrageous
Or soon you will discover
That after a night out partying
You need a whole week to recover

Tip
Both these
ages can be
replaced

My darling daughter it's a pleasure
To give you these birthday wishes
Your gift today, I'm pleased to say
Is that you don't have to do the dishes

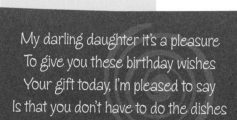

When I heard you were twenty-four
I fainted and hit the floor
For with all of your wrinkles
And your fair share of crinkles
I thought you were fifty or more

Tip
Twenty-four
can be replaced
with thirty-four,
forty-four
etc.

As you grow older
you're becoming
more attractive,
sensitive clever and
lovable every day...
you're slowly
turning into me!!!

Just because your hair is grey
And your veins are all dark blue
Doesn't mean we won't come out
And celebrate with you

It's such a special occasion
I want to shout 'Happy Birthday!'
But I needn't bother
You wouldn't hear me anyway

You love your golf, it's your true mistress
It always makes you glad
If I ever said you couldn't go
Then you'd go putting mad

In your early years
You were quite naughty
Then later you were mean
But now you're simply perfect
You're super sweet sixteen

Now that you've reached the grand age of 18
You probably want to sink a pint or three
But I started drinking at 18
And look at the state of me

With hammer and saw and utility belt
You're Mr DIY
Everything you make might fall apart
But at least you give it a try

You're a real rock legend
An air guitar playing dude
For hard riffs and killer solos
You're always in the mood

My brother is so nerdy
A real computer geek
So I've set him a birthday challenge
To explore the real world for a week!

You've accessories in every colour
Your handbag collection's space defying
And yet it's set to grow and grow
Because you can't stop buying

You're strictly the coolest of the cool
You bring the girls to their knees
In fact you are so very cool
I'm afraid your friends might freeze

You've always got
your eyes in a book
The pages are wrapped round
Your head
So on your birthday
Give your eyes a rest
And read this rhyme instead

If it hasn't got an engine
It's simply not for you
Well tough
I've just bought this card
And it will have to do

Most things your age are past their prime
They're spoilt or going mouldy
But you're still going
From strength to strength
You super golden oldie

I'd hate to be 21
All that youth, energy and fun
It must be horrific
To feel that terrific
I'm so happy I'm not young!

I can tell you're now a teenager
That racket you play is infernal
You never wash, you lay about
And you're starting to become
nocturnal

Tip
All three of
these sports can
be changed to suit
the recipient's
sporting
preferences

Footie, rugby and basketball
You really are sports mad
You hate it when the season ends
But that's the bit that makes me glad

Birthday Celebrations

There are no magic potions
That can stop Father Time
No creams or lotions
That will have you looking fine
Now you've turned fifty
There's no going back
You'll never be as nifty
Now that Father Time's attacked

Time waits for no man...so how come you are 21 again

Have you considered plastic surgery
It's practical and fun
For although your thighs will still look sixty
Your face will look twenty-one

To think of the best birthday present
I searched my heart and soul
And then decided what you'd really want
Is a day with the remote control

When you were young
You had a full head of hair
But now that you're older it's going
Just buy a wig to go out on the town
And then your new locks will be flowing

You look like a fop
In your velvet top
With your sequinned patterns
Upon each sock
Your fashion is bold
And incredibly old
And out of a
different epoch

I heard you've
turned faulty
(40)... I've known
that for ages

You're getting very old now
And yet you look just fine
I guess you get better as you mature
Just like a good red wine

I love going shopping
For your birthday card
Walking round the shops with glee
Because after I've got
Your birthday card
I can get something else for me

Now that you're thirty
Stop being flirty
You're not as young as you feel
You'll need some slippers, a pipe
And an early night
Now that you're over the hill

Birthdays are great for the presents and fun
And all the wine and beer
But it means that I get another year older
So I think I'll skip mine this year

How could I forget your birthday?
I'm an absolute disgrace
Hopefully next year
I'll have birthday cake in my mouth
Rather than egg all over my face

If I had a pound for every birthday you'd had, I'd have more money that you'd like to admit!

23

Birthday Celebrations

My mind must be going,
I must be getting old,
I always get the dates wrong,
And forget what I've been told
So here's belated birthday wishes,
And there's no need to fear,
For you can be sure that I won't forget
To send you a card next year

Happy Birthday

I got myself in a kerfuffle
I was confused, bemused and perplexed
I'm always getting my dates wrong
Don't know the difference from one day to the next
I'm always mixed up, muddled and disordered
My mind is going you see
So I'm sorry I forgot your birthday
I'm as stupid as stupid can be

I've heard you've got a bun in the oven
And I'm delighted that's a fact
You'll soon know the joys
Of dirty nappies and toys
And the feeling of sick on your back

Congratulations on your new baby, in just a few short months it will be wetting itself, crying and dribbling... and then just a few years after that it'll think it knows best!

I'm so happy to hear
That you're going to be a Daddy and Mummy
And with us in the family you're sure
To never be short of a dummy

Thank goodness you were pregnant...

I thought you had just let yourself go.

The cost of having a baby
Is nothing short of crazy
But don't let the price go to your head
Or else you'll start thinking
That the cash could be spent
On a flash new car instead

Having a new child can pose problems: they are messy, they don't know when they smell and they are totally dependent on you...it's a bit like having a husband.

I'd love to be a baby
So I could be naughty and rude
I could sleep all day
And throw my food
I wouldn't have to go to work
Or even get up at all
Being an adult is overrated
It's a baby's life for me

Your new baby is so innocent
It copies everything you do
It doesn't yet realise
That it's already as clever as you

Tip
'it' can be
replaced with
'he' or 'she'

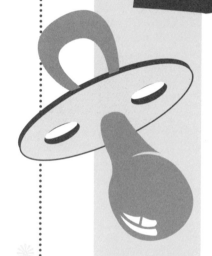

You've got a beautiful baby
That everyone adores
In fact it's so gorgeous
I don't think it's yours

Crying and whining and nappies
Can give you the baby blues
But as we don't have to deal with it
We're thrilled to hear your good news

I want to see your new delivery
Play with him and hold him too
But when he needs his nappy changed
I'll pass him back to you

Love is
in the Air

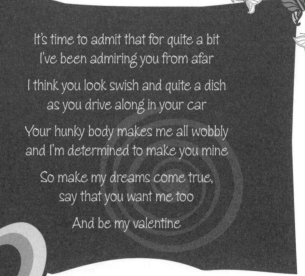

It's time to admit that for quite a bit
I've been admiring you from afar

I think you look swish and quite a dish
as you drive along in your car

Your hunky body makes me all wobbly
and I'm determined to make you mine

So make my dreams come true,
say that you want me too

And be my valentine

You're definitely an alpha male, an Adonis there's no doubt
I want to hold you in my arms and then to the world I'd shout
'I've got the perfect specimen, he's the best man in the world'
And there's no chance of him leaving me coz I'm the perfect girl

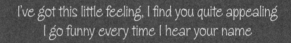

I've got this little feeling, I find you quite appealing
I go funny every time I hear your name

See it's my heart that you've been stealing
And I'll be dancing on the ceiling

If you tell me that you feel the same

So don't be dull and boring, it's you that I'm adoring
I'll show you a time that'll never be forgot

Quit all your ignoring and together we'll be soaring
get with me and I'll show you what I've got

If I were Jane and you were Tarzan
then through the jungle we'd swing

We'd live a life of blissful peace
and not want for anything

But we don't live in a jungle
where we jump from tree to tree

Which is a shame coz I quite fancy
you going wild with me

Happy Valentines

Drop me a line,
be my valentine

I'll give you my hugs
and my kissing

I've got this and more
All set in store

You don't know what
You've been missing!

You're my Angelina Jolie and I'm your Brad Pitt

You're a super stunner and I'm super fit

We're so very trendy and we dress to impress

In fact I'm sure it won't be long until we're fighting off the press

Tip
these names
can be changed
to whoever
you like

Cupid shot an arrow
and I knew that you
were for me

So let me show you
a good time and I'm
sure that you'll
agree!

I bought you
a big box of
chocolates but
decided not to
give you them
in case you ate
them all and got
fat!

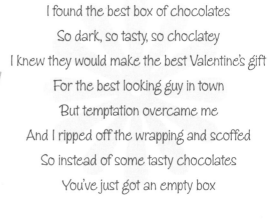

I found the best box of chocolates

So dark, so tasty, so choclatey

I knew they would make the best Valentine's gift

For the best looking guy in town

But temptation overcame me

And I ripped off the wrapping and scoffed

So instead of some tasty chocolates

You've just got an empty box

I love you for your fantastic looks
I love you because you're funny
I love you because you treat me right
And you're worth lots of money

When you smile and take my hand
My feelings you can't understand
I go all sweaty
My legs turn to spaghetti
And I start thinking of confetti

For Valentine's Day I'm going to take you out
And it's love I'll make you feel
You just have to decide if you'd prefer
Chicken nuggets
Or a burger meal

When I first saw you, Cupid shot me with his arrow... luckily he was arrested and I'm pressing charges

On Valentine's Day it would be easy to spend
Lots of money on chocolates and flowers
But I know you'll be happy
With gifts not so tacky
And get your present in the midnight hours

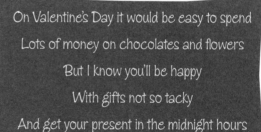

Let's scrap the flowers and balloons
And all the tiresome chase
Why don't you just come out with me
And let me snog your face

Love can conquer countries
Love can raise you from the floor
If love would do the dishes
I'd like being in love even more

You're always cool and trendy
Everyone wants you for their Valentine
And I'm afraid that I'm no different
So come and say that you'll be mine

Every time I see
you my heart
skips a beat...
which is really
dangerous if I
see you a lot!

I heard you're getting married
With a love so true and bold
The news left me happy, but wistful
Because it makes me feel so old

After all these years of nodding and winking
And not-so-subtle suggestion
We're thrilled that the romantic fool
Has finally popped the question

Saying yes is the easy bit
Proposing is just the start you see
Just wait til it comes to wedding plans
And you'll see what divas you can be

It's meant to be a special occasion
When he goes down on one knee
I'm not romantic, but I do it often
It's the back pain that gets me you see

We thought it would never happen
We can't believe it's true
How could anybody fall
For an ugly mug like you

In years when you see your wedding video
You'll see how happy you are
And you'll notice your loving glances
From near and from afar

But as you watch your wedding video
You'll find yourself staring
At all your lovely guests
And the ridiculous clothes they were wearing

Enjoy this bliss and romance
And do take the chance
To bask in what people say
Because you'll have no rest
But plenty of stress
When you start to plan your big day

It's clear that you're perfect for each other
You two are peas in a pod
It's not that you're both graceful and charming
But rather clumsy and odd

Now the question's been popped
There's no time to stop
Let's get in a wedding planner
You'll want only the best
Regardless of cost
So you can wed in a very posh manner

I was enraged when
you got engaged

This simply will not do

Although you might stay together
forever and ever

I had my eye on you

When I got engaged it was a wonderful day
I wanted to shout and sing
Not because I'd tied up my man
But coz of the diamond on the ring

If you want a massive wedding
But can't afford the fee
Just sell exclusive picture rights
To a tacky magazine

After sharing your lives for so long
It's great to hear the news
Just make sure when you share a bank account
The money doesn't go on shoes

If he's done his homework
And he's bought the best around
Then your new engagement ring
Should be weighing your left arm down

I said you were good together
And you set each other's world alight
Now you've finally got engaged
It's great once again to be right

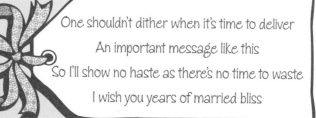

One shouldn't dither when it's time to deliver
An important message like this
So I'll show no haste as there's no time to waste
I wish you years of married bliss

From the moment you looked in each other's eyes
It was clear you were bewitched
And now just a couple of months later
You've announced you're getting hitched

Congratulations on your engagement!

You're both sure to both look wonderful
On your wedding day
The stunning dress, the dapper suit
The beautiful bouquet
But as you stroll down the aisle
And prepare to say 'I do'
You'll feel strangely jealous
Coz I'll look better than both of you

I get all emotional at weddings
At yours i'm bound to cry
And I can't hold in the tears
No matter how much I try
So if you see me welling up
I'm not sad or feeling blue
I just get teary at weddings
But i'm really happy for you!

Some people marry for love
Others marry for money
But the only reason you're marrying each other
Is because you both look funny

Wedding bells are ringing
Your rings are truly blinging
You look the perfect couple
So let's have a celebration
To recognise the elation
As we wish the best to both of you

There's rings and things, suits and boots
Speeches, champagne and wine
There's a cake to make and dancing to do
I hope you have an amazing time

Roses are red
Violets are blue
And so will your nose be
If you don't say 'I do'

With stressful speeches
And annoying relatives
For both bride and groom
At least after all the fuss
You've got the honeymoon

You need something old, something new
Something borrowed and something blue
Well I am old, but my outfit is new
You've borrowed lots of money
So your big day won't be blue

We've been looking forward to your wedding for so long
It seems a shame it has to end
Is there any chance you could get divorced
And do it all over again?

The highlights of weddings are obvious
You'll have a great day to be sure
But you'll come crashing down with a bump
When you realise you have a mother-in-law

Build up your gift list nice and long
With things for both bride and groom
That way you'll come back to fantastic presents
After your honeymoon

At your wedding you both looked wonderful
It's clear you spent hours getting it right
But after looking so good all day long
I bet you couldn't wait for the wedding night

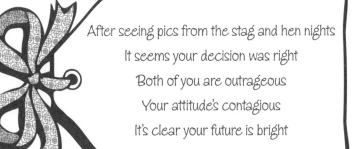

After seeing pics from the stag and hen nights
It seems your decision was right
Both of you are outrageous
Your attitude's contagious
It's clear your future is bright

We're true soul mates, we'll always be together
Even when we are all old and sagging
I'll love you forever, you're my true love
If only you'd stop with your nagging

I'm dashing, charming and handsome
I fill you with giggles and glee
With all of my charms who could blame you
For falling for a man like me

Even in the morning I'm stunning
I catch glances from near and afar
So happy anniversary darling
I can only imagine how happy you are

Happy anniversary Mum and Dad
You truly are a perfect couple
But we're still putting you in a home when you're older
No matter how much you struggle

Not for all the tea in China nor all the pizza in Rome
Not for all the haggis in Scotland nor all the texts on your mobile phone
Not for all the tacos in Mexico nor the sushi in Japan
Would I ever give you up on you you'll always be my man

Tip
'man' can be
replaced with
'woman', or
even 'love' or
one

I fell in love with your sense of humour
With your kindness, laughter and grace
But I still can't quite be persuaded
To fall in love with the wrinkles on your face

There are a lot of ugly people in the world today
They're not blessed with the fine looks that you have on display
There are a lot of nasty people, the kind that I avoid
They don't have your wit and charm, which is to be enjoyed
There are a lot of stupid people, who haven't got a clue
And I'm afraid to say I'm one of them because I've become a fool for you

If we were rich I'd take you dancing
And we'd have some well posh grub
But we're not so we're off to the chippy
And then we'll end up in the pub

You've got no super powers
You can't fly or leap tall walls
You certainly don't have super strength
Or any strength at all

But you'll always be my hero
In a funny kind of way
Because you're always the one who saves me
Each and every day

Some people impress with their looks
Others because they are funny
I went with you because I'd had a glass or two
And you said you had lots of money

Getting into a relationship is often fun and exciting

Getting to know your partner can be thrilling and enticing

But it's difficult as the years go by and things become more boring

That's why we admire you for staying together

And putting up with each others snoring

Happy Anniversary

Sometimes I want to scream at you
Because you annoy me so
But I just can't walk away from you
So I wanted you to know

Even though we shout and fight
And even though you're annoying
And drive me round the bend
We're always sure to
Make up in the end

Neither of you are lookers
You've got uglier as you've grown
Thank god you have each other
Or you'd both be on your own

I've learnt that when a couple
have shared years of married bliss

They prefer you to be courteous
rather than take the... mick

Happy
Anniversary

Don't ever think of yourself as useless
As stupid, rude or ugly
For you can always make yourself feel better
These things are relative you see

You'll always be the best looking girl in the house
The cleverest one on our settee
You'll always be the nicest lady in our street
The prettiest girl that's married to me!

Why not get a
new car for your
wife – if the
dealers will
accept the trade

Tip
wife can be
changed to
husband

You're the perfect couple
You're never sad or blue
When I get married
I want to be like you

The secret of a happy marriage
Is love and trust and sharing
Always let him watch the football
And say she looks nice in what she's wearing

Tip
Football
can be
substituted

'I do' doesn't mean 'I'll do everything'

You're a golden couple there's no doubt
You two have certainly got some clout
You've lasted so many years
Through both joy and tears
You're what relationships are all about

It was clear the night I met my dear that I was bound to fall in love
You were the best, finely dressed, and surely sent down from above
And the day we met I'll never forget
Because you made my life complete
I'm so pleased that when I went down on one knee
You didn't beat a hasty retreat

Your wedding's still fresh in your mind
But I bet you're disappointed to find
That after all that expense and caper
This year's marked only with paper

Never criticise her faults. It's probably those faults that kept her from getting a better husband.

A ruby is a precious gem
And you're a precious pair
It would be fitting to buy you a ruby
But I haven't the cash to spare

Tip
'ruby' can be replaced with 'sapphire', 'diamond', etc

When I told my husband he should be more affectionate on our wedding anniversary he got a second wife!

This anniversary is marked by tin
10 years together it's been
Let's hope your marriage remains
When she's got varicose veins
And his hair is starting to thin

You two are such romantics
Now you celebrate your pearl
He's the perfect boy
And she's the perfect girl

And as you grow older
May your love burn like a flame
Even when you're old and ugly
And you forget each other's name

Happy 30th Anniversary

Twenty years together is certainly not minor
It's traditional that I mark it with China
So if you come round here swift
I've got the perfect gift
A Chinese meal for two of which there's no finer

Happy China wedding anniversary

Friends
& Family

With kindness, compassion
And a love of good fashion
It's clear you have a special blend
But you're weird and crazy, funny and zany
And that's why you're such a special friend

The hardest thing about being your friend is keeping all the secrets you tell me

There's always gossip to gossip about
and there's always gossip to hear
And we've gossiped about so much gossip
each and every year
And the time flies when you're gossiping
And we've been gossiping till our lips go numb
And I think that we will be gossiping
For many years to come

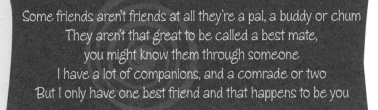

Some friends aren't friends at all they're a pal, a buddy or chum
They aren't that great to be called a best mate,
you might know them through someone
I have a lot of companions, and a comrade or two
But I only have one best friend and that happens to be you

You've always been there when I need you
You've always leant a helping hand
So I wanted to say how much I care
And can I borrow a couple of grand?

A true friend is the sort of person who doesn't think a secret is something they can tell just one person!

You are
my friend, my ally, my pal

And I hope it continues
till you're a right old gal!

Life is like a boxing match
And sometimes you're on the ropes
That's when you need someone in your corner
Telling you not to give up hope
I know you'll always be there for me
So I can come out swinging
And with you on my side I know that this
Is a match that I'm capable of winning

You're definitely my best friend
Our times together are always good
You put up with me even though I don't call
As often as I should

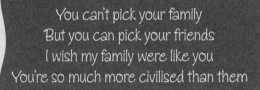

You can't pick your family
But you can pick your friends
I wish my family were like you
You're so much more civilised than them

BE ST
FRI END

I hope you'll always be my friend
Because I'm sure there will always be
Chick flicks at the cinema
That our husbands don't want to see

We've been friends since we were little
And I guess not much has changed
Apart from we've got old and wrinkly
And our faces looks rearranged

Dancing to cheesy tunes
Round our handbags on the floor
Growing old disgracefully
We'll be friends forevermore

As best friends I know it's the trend
To do everything as a two
But you have to face it
that I want some space
When I need to go to the loo

I've heard that
friends should
stay friends
through thick and
thin... well you're
thick and I'm
still your friend!

The great thing about a friend like you
Is it doesn't matter what I do
I could call you a relic
And you'd still be angelic
And not leave me looking black and blue

You've stuck with me through thick and thin
You've been there when you should
And I'm so annoying and frustrating
I don't know anyone else that would

You'll always be my best friend
And I'll scorn those who knock it
For years we'll continue to chat
And live in each other's pocket

I can always count on a friend like you... by the way can I borrow some money?

Mum, you crazy party animal,
You love to dance and sing

And I know that on this Mother's Day
You'll be getting in the swing

So let's go out and have a drink or two
Because you're my best friend too

And I'm sure by the end of the night
I'll be in as bad a state as you

'Sit back from the TV',
'You're not wearing that',
'Be back by half past nine'
'Turn the lights off'
'We're not made of money'
You'd tell me all the time

These phrases that you've repeated
To me will never be forgot
And I'll know you'll always be there
To give your advice
Whether I want it or not

Happy Mother's Day

Mum, you're simply perfect, you never miss a beat
You give so much to all of us and make our lives complete
You've always been there for me
And cheered me up when I've been sad
But i'm so very different, I must take after dad!

The gods had a meeting
And with the best ingredients compiled
They created the perfect mother
And now you've got the perfect child

You are my rock, you've been there
Through rain and stormy weather
And I can't think of a better thank you
Than going shopping together!

Mother, you're still my best friend
Even though you drive me round the bend
And despite your bad hearing
So much of you is endearing
Especially the money you lend

Happy Mother's Day

You're caring, loving, compassionate
You've always been the same
You're the best mother anyone could want
If you'd just stop forgetting my name

Mum, since moving out
I've missed all your caring
And I can't help but think
There's things we should be sharing

So on this Mother's Day
I've got some presents for you
I've brought a pile of washing
And some dirty dishes too

Mum, I know you miss me
And you miss the things I do
So I've messed your house up
Just like when I was living with you

Friends & Family

Whenever we come round
You're offering us food and drink
So this Mother's Day it's about time
We waited on you I think

Forget about the stress and work
It's time to have a fun day
Why not stop all your worrying
On this Mothering Sunday

My mum's the best
She's there for me
And I love to go round and see her
And with all the flowers I've brought for her
It's a good job she doesn't have hayfever

Mother, I love you although you're old
And starting to creak
I just wish you wouldn't still spit on tissues
And rub them on my cheek

My dearest mother, I would have no other
But I might make a change here or two
I'd give you more money
So you wouldn't look at me funny
When I ask for a loan off of you

Friends & Family

75

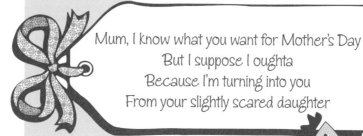

Mum, I know what you want for Mother's Day
But I suppose I oughta
Because I'm turning into you
From your slightly scared daughter

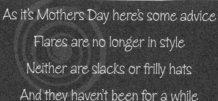

As it's Mothers Day here's some advice
Flares are no longer in style
Neither are slacks or frilly hats
And they haven't been for a while

On Mother's Day it's great to write cards

To give you esteem and praise

It would take ages to tell you

Because you can't hear a thing these days

Tip
This could
be changed
for Dad

Mum, you raised me and I'll think you'll agree

You did a pretty good job

So happy Mother's Day, you're perfect by the way

From the perfect little girl

You shout at the TV, you don't cook or clean

You burp and then scratch your bum

Yet I'm still happy to be your daughter

I'm just relieved that I take after mum

Happy Father's Day

Dad, you're a workaholic
Trying to give your family the best
So why not celebrate this Father's Day
By sitting down and having a rest

I've simply got the best dad

That anyone could have had

He's taught me all he's ever known

And now that I've grown

We are both totally mad

Dad, you're a football addict
You're always watching the stuff
Whether its premier league or conference
It's clear that you can't get enough
You're always watching the sports news
And the score updates on the TV
The only problem with your addiction
Is that you seem to have passed it to me

Dad, I'm your mirror image
You've taught me how to avoid chores
So that's why my garden isn't mown
It's just the same as yours

Happy Father's Day

Dad, as it's Father's Day
You need to be treated right
You should be first in the bathroom
Without needing to have a fight

Mum should be waiting on you
In every single way
In fact these 24 hours
Should be just like any other day

Dad, for Father's Day we should go for a meal
Or perhaps to see a posh show
I was going to book a cab for the night
But you're the only taxi service I know

I know you like your peace and quiet
Enjoy your space at home
So as a present this Father's Day
We are all going to leave you alone

Dad, Happy Father's Day
I love you though we're nothing alike
In fact Nan says I look like the postman
Who used to visit each day on his bike

Father, you're the world to me
You'll always be in my good books
Not just because I inherited your charm
But also your fiendish good looks

When you were younger
You and Mum were richer
You were filled with happiness and glee
Now there's a picture of me in your wallet
Where your money used to be

Happy Father's Day

You taught me how to shave and ride a bike like you... No wonder I've got cuts on my face and need stabilizers too

We both know Mum rules the
roost and she always gets her way

Here's to the one day every year
She might listen to what you say

I've made an extra special effort
On this Father's Day
I shaved off all my hair
So you could use it as a toupee

Dad, I modelled
myself on you...
just let me
watch the footie
before I sign
this card

Never raise a hand to your kids... it leaves the rest of your body unprotected

Dad, you taught me a lesson
when I was young
About women
and holding my tongue
Well I don't mean to sound mad
but that advice was bad
Because now my partner
nags more than mum

Dad, I'm turning into you
There's nothing I can do
I'm going grey
My style's gone away
And I'm growing ear hair too

As it's Father's Day,
I'm sure I should say
How you're wonderful
and age defying
How you've got such grace,
and a non-wrinkly face
But I don't want
to be accused of lying

I'm off the hook, I'm uncontrollable
I'm going slightly mad
When people ask what's wrong with me
I tell them I got it from my Dad

All Change

I know you really want to go
Explore some pastures new
But we're all afraid that when you leave
It will show how little WE do

We tried to tunnel under the fence
and sneak past security
We even scaled down the drainpipe
in our desperate bid to be free
But somehow you've done it
and we'll miss you there's no doubt
Now you've escaped from this charming place ...
can you tell us how to get out!

When we heard
you were leaving
we didn't know
how we would
replace you...
luckily we found
a cheap coffee
machine on eBay!

You're moving up, new office, new desk
Your promotion is surely due
But we wonder if the new people there
Will annoy you the way that we do

The best thing about having a new job
isn't the wage or all the perks
It's certainly not more holiday
or not having to work with us jerks
The most satisfying thing about a new job
and it's sure to give you a grin
It's seeing your boss's horrified face
when you hand your notice in

The gods of business that live on high
have shined their light on you
They've noticed your dedication
and all that work you do
So now it's time to rise through the ranks
and complete your job ascension
And we're all stunned because we thought
the bosses weren't paying attention

You're soon to be raking in loads of cash
and driving luxury cars

You'll be showing off your swish new phone
and hanging out in trendy bars

But as you move to your new job
don't forget this little crew

Or we'll tell your new employers
about all the work you didn't do

We know you want out
it's a new job you need

And leaving is your preference

But you do so much work,
we want you to stay

So we gave you
a really bad reference

I know you work harder than me
I can hear your pencil scribbling
And your fingers tapping at your keyboard
Your thumbs are never twiddling
You've shown me up for so long now
And I wanted you to know
That although I'm sure to miss you
I won't be sad to see you go

Your new job will be demanding
You'll need your knowledge and your drive
And use them both to work out
When the best time is to skive

I don't wish to cause a commotion
About your new promotion
But it's clear you're in for a big pay rise
And while your stock is rising
It's true I won't be disguising
The fact that we have such friendly ties

You're moving on because you're good
And I would never doubt it
But while you were doing all the work
I was getting out of it

Work is no laughing matter... but now that you're off I can't stop giggling

We're stunned at the job that you've landed
You're going to leave us all stranded
But we have our suspicions
How you got that position
We think the deal was somewhat back-handed

In your new job, here's some friendly advice
To keep you out of mischief with your recruiter
If anything goes wrong or fails at work
Just blame it on your computer

You're irreplaceable, that's probably why you were never promoted

Ambition is a poor excuse for not having enough sense to be lazy

We're like a pack of hyenas
Just waiting for you to leave
When you're gone we'll get into your desk
And all the good stationery we will thieve

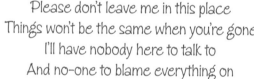

When we said
you couldn't
leave we didn't
mean it
figuratively...
we've let your
tyres down

Please don't leave me in this place
Things won't be the same when you're gone
I'll have nobody here to talk to
And no-one to blame everything on

Now that we've heard you're leaving, the race has begun
I've got dibbs on your desk and chair and your stapling gun
Someone's claimed all your stationery and your PC
It is a shame you're leaving, but at least there's more stuff for me

We're so sorry that you're leaving
You mean the world to us
But we know that you're quite private
And don't like a lot of fuss

So I only got a skywriter
To spell out your name
And we went and hired a circus
If it's all the same

We're putting on some fireworks
And we've arranged a gourmet meal
Because we're so sad you're going
And you should know the way we feel

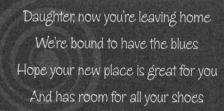

Daughter, now you're leaving home
We're bound to have the blues
Hope your new place is great for you
And has room for all your shoes

Just because you're leaving
You should not be grieving
You know you won't be on your own
In fact you'll be moaning
That I don't stop phoning
And you want me to leave you alone

You should know we don't want you to go

Because in the end we all know

That without you here

Dragging your rear

Our decent hard work won't show

We know you're off somewhere else
and there's nothing we can do
But we have got some happy news,
we're coming with you too
So just when you thought it was over
and good-bye you'd have to tell
Just as we are here for you,
we'll also be there as well

Sometimes the grass is greener on the other side
You have to swim a different ocean and feel a different tide
But keep that grass mown and that ocean clear
Or it could end up being just as bad as here

It's ever so easy
To feel a little queasy
When you're off to do something new
But it would be thick
To feel so sick
Especially for someone as special as you

We hear you talking about leaving
But we are disbelieving
Because we don't think you can stand the flack
And one you've said your good byes
It's great here you'll soon realize
And it wont be long before you're rushing back

Your leaving has
made me quite
unhappy...
it accentuates
the fact that
I'm still here

What a fantastic feeling
Handing in your resignation letter
Even if I were promoted
I don't think I'd feel any better

All Change

After clawing your way up the ladder you've finally decided to jump off...
Happy Retirement

Now you're off on your retirement
To travel near and far
As you're having fun remember us
We can't tell you how jealous we are

I'm so sorry that you're leaving,
you'll never be replaced

But the lessons that you've taught us
will not go to waste

With the wisdom that you've passed on
this place will never be the same

And we're all sure that we'll never do
a hard day's work again

100

Retiring must be a great feeling
Must make you feel so alive
It's one of the only things
I'm looking forward to about being 65

I feel like you're leaving to run away from your problems... good idea, can I come?

You're leaving to have a baby
You're clearly up the duff
I can't believe you want the stress of a child
The stress of this place should be enough

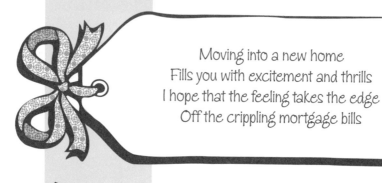

Moving into a new home
Fills you with excitement and thrills
I hope that the feeling takes the edge
Off the crippling mortgage bills

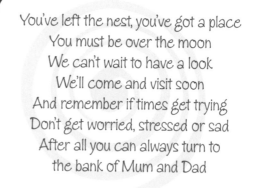

You've left the nest, you've got a place
You must be over the moon
We can't wait to have a look
We'll come and visit soon
And remember if times get trying
Don't get worried, stressed or sad
After all you can always turn to
the bank of Mum and Dad

I don't know why you moved out,
you had it sweet at home
You could lie around for hours
and always use the phone
You had no responsibility,
you needn't cook or clean
You could leave your washing everywhere
and it would turn up pristine
But now you've found your own place
I bet you'll be sad to go
Especially when your first bill arrives
or when you have to wash your own clothes

You've finally found a new home, a place to settle down
A place where you can argue, while no one else is around

Congratulations on your new home

Beware the DIY shop
Beware the furniture shops too
When they find out you have a new home
They'll take all your money from you

I'm quite the interior designer you know
And I'm willing to do your new home
I can do any style, I'm extremely worthwhile
I'll have it looking like Paris or Rome

Unless you're disgusted by beds
(Jewel encrusted)
And purple drapes in the hall
Then my skills will be of use,
I shan't take an excuse
I will wait by the phone for your call

Congrats on the new home

It's easy to be KOI of the housing market
You need to TACKLE the whole thing with grace
We just thank COD you've now moved in
And you've found a really nice PLAICE

Buying a place can be frustrating
But when you get there it's elating
But the joy and the cheer
Turns to boredom and fear
When you see how much needs decorating

When you walk into your new home
You'll want to make it your own
But all your money will be spent
On bills and on rent
So those designs you'll have to postpone

All Change

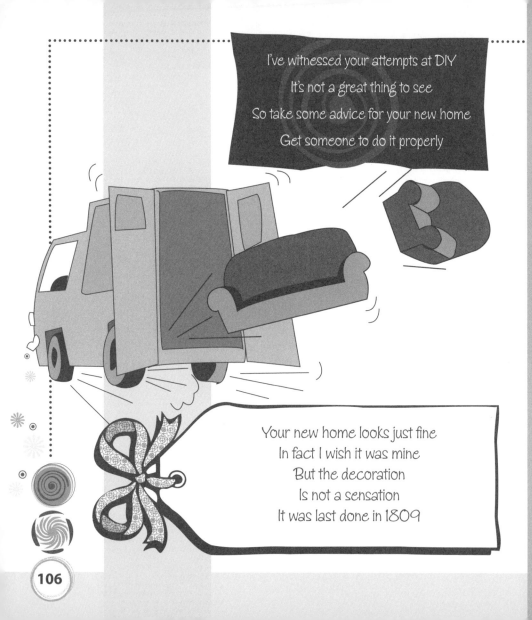

I've witnessed your attempts at DIY
It's not a great thing to see
So take some advice for your new home
Get someone to do it properly

Your new home looks just fine
In fact I wish it was mine
But the decoration
Is not a sensation
It was last done in 1809

When you get a house it's such a shame
You have to play the flatpack game
It's full of riddles and puzzles galore
You'll have all the parts spread out on the floor

But it won't make sense and you'll be brought to your knees
By the complex instruction book in Chinese
And when it's finished after a five day slog
It won't look like it did in the catalogue

You've got so much stuff, that you'll find it tough

Getting it to your new place

You'll need two vans

And hundreds of hands

Let's hope your new home has the space

Party, Party, Party

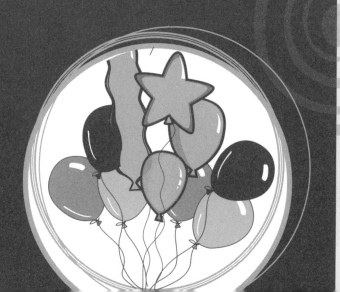

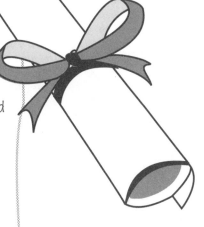

There's no doubt that you're an Einstein
A genius of the highest kind
With test results like these
You'll soon be appearing on Mastermind

You'll be winning Nobel prizes
And wowing experts with your thinking
But that's all in the future
First let's make some time for drinking

Congratulations on your exam results

You examined every exam
And delved deep into every question
Your studious studying paid off
And now you're almost too clever to mention

As you throw your mortarboard in the air
And celebrate your degree
Be sure it doesn't fall and hit you
Or you'll look as silly as me

With a brain as big as a small country
You're bound to be a sensation
The future's bright so take a bow
And enjoy your graduation

Well Done

After all the nervousness and tension
Revising from night till noon
It appears you are a clever clogs
You'll be teaching your teachers soon

We've heard the news and it appears
It's a time of congratulation
If we could we'd stand and applaud
To give you a roaring ovation

That truly is amazing, it's clear that you need praising
You've become a star through and through
We were at first confounded, then utterly astounded
So huge congratulations are clearly due

Congratulations on first place
You must have a smug smile on your face

Before your exams I thought you were thick
Now that you've passed them I feel quite sick
For all my laughing at your stupidity
It turns out that you're more clever than me

After years of studying at uni
The real world can make you feel puny
But with results like these
You'll soon be a big cheese
With an office that's both posh and roomy

Its easy to poke and make fun
When the test has not yet begun
But you worked hard all along
And proved us all wrong
So we feel obliged to tell you'well done'

You battled and you worked at it
And now you made it through
We would have given up by now
So well done, good for you

You've passed your examinations
This calls for congratulations
Surely you're the cleverest there can be
All these genius presentations
Go to serve as confirmations
That you'll soon be using long words just like me

You did so well
to pass your
exams...
especially as
five out of every
four people
have trouble
with maths

As you were speeding around that corner
And knocked that pedestrian down
I'm amazed your driving examiner
Didn't mark you down
And I don't know what you said
That made him pass your test
But we're so happy for you
So congratulations on your success

It's great that you've passed your driving test
But the cost will drive you mental
You'll end up selling your car
Just to afford the petrol

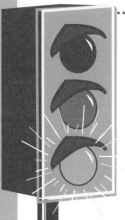

Congratulations

Driving lessons seem to wear off
After you have passed your test
You too will find yourself not indicating
Just like all the rest

Now you've passed your driving test
Even more skills will arrive
For you never really learn to swear
Until the day you learn to drive

Now you've passed your driving test
You'll be driving near and far
The only question that I have is
Will you clean the car?

Good luck on your new venture
All the best we wish to you
Now you can annoy other people
In many pastures new

Good luck you brave old chap
I know that you'll see it through
Just remember that I'm your best mate
When it all goes right for you

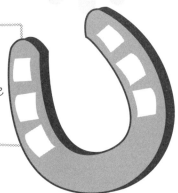

Interviews are difficult
And some questions may be tough
But if you're getting nervous
Just imagine them in the buff

Good luck on your driving test
Don't get your knickers in a twist
And if the examiner's really nasty
Introduce him to your fist

You're a clever chap there's no doubt
About your exam results I want to shout
But now you're off to uni
With a timetable that's puny
You can enjoy being a layabout

Good luck at university

We'll be wishing you the best of luck
As you go into your big day
However you do, you can rest assured
You're much better than me anyway

Life's a series of roads and hurdles
That take you to a wondrous places
Here's hoping that you get to paradise
While others fall on their faces

Some of us are daring
and want to take a chance
The rest of us just sit back
offering an occasional glance
You're a true pioneer
not afraid to get into the muck
So while we're watching from afar
we'll all be wishing you good luck

Wishing you good luck
All seems rather lame
Because you ace everything you do
And this will be the same

I'd offer you my good luck pants
But there's no need to be superstitious
Because you're success is so proficient
I've started to become suspicious

Wishing you the
best of luck...
just don't
outshine me

I don't want to wish you good luck
Because you're doing as well as you dare
In fact if you got yet more good luck
Some might consider it unfair

It's time to take your skill
and put it to the test
With my good luck on your side
I'm sure you'll show the rest

Sweaty palms and nervousness
It's time to put them aside
Let me do the worrying for you
So you can take it all in your stride

We'll be superstitious for you
So you just use your skill and focus
Concentrate on impressing
While we use our hocus-pocus

Thanks very much for the invite
I'd be delighted to come along
If you should need to find me
I'll be by the buffet, where I belong

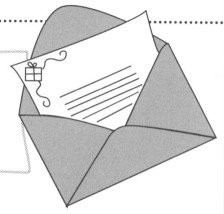

I can't wait for your wedding
It's so nice of you to invite me
I hope my pink tuxedo and chrome shoes
Won't look too unsightly

I think my trendy disco dancing
Will be sure to cause some 'wows'
Especially if I start to breakdance
As you exchange your vows

So thanks for the invite
I'm sure you won't regret
As I'm going to make your wedding
A day that you'll never forget

We're going on a hen night
it's bound to be outrageous
The fun and anticipation
seems to be contagious
We're feeling the need to get dressed
and then act quite salacious
Let's hope by the time your wedding day comes
you won't be so flirtatious

This is an invitation to a wonderful sensation
My party will be fantastic make no mistake
But be warned I'll throw you out if I have any doubt
That you're only there to eat my birthday cake

I've got a little event coming up
I'm having a little do
There will be cakes and presents and alcohol
And hopefully there will be you!

Thanks for the invitation
We're coming, make no mistake
We're looking forward to sharing your day
And then eating all your cake

I want to invite you to a feast,
A date that's well worth booking
But unfortunately it won't be great
Because I'm doing all the cooking

Please come to my BBQ

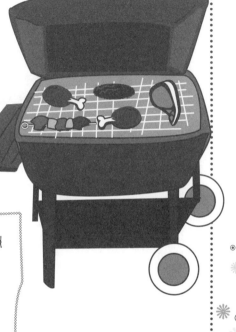

She's the sweetest woman in the world
And now you have the chance
To gaze upon her in wonder
Or offer her a dance
And for this her special day
A party we are throwing
Don't miss this opportunity
Be sure that you are going

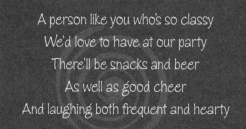

A person like you who's so classy
We'd love to have at our party
There'll be snacks and beer
As well as good cheer
And laughing both frequent and hearty

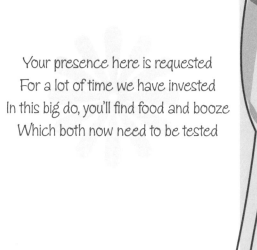

Your presence here is requested
For a lot of time we have invested
In this big do, you'll find food and booze
Which both now need to be tested

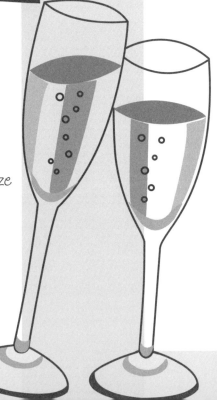

While she's single, we can all mingle
It's a chance to see a stripper or two
So don't miss this date
Come out with your mate
'Before she says her 'I do'

It's time for the stag do
To get in a state that's unflattering
See some strippers, have some laughs
And give your livers a battering

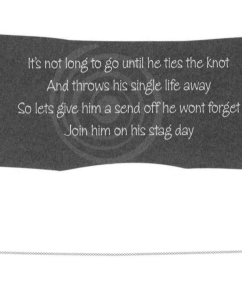

It's not long to go until he ties the knot
And throws his single life away
So lets give him a send off he wont forget
Join him on his stag day

Weddings are beautiful and romantic
Not the place to drink, sweat and swear
So why not do this at the stag do
And help us to shave off his hair

Tip
Substitute 'his' for the groom's name in the last line.

This party is bound to be splendid
My hosting will be commended
So say you'll be here
And bring good cheer
Or else I'll be offended

We've got a new house
Me and the spouse
Now we're having a celebration
If you want us to be nice
Here's some advice
Bring some wine with this invitation

Thanks a lot, cheers for that
I don't know what to say
You shouldn't have, but I'm glad you did
You've really made my day

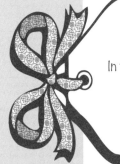

That was such a nice gesture
Such a wonderful thing to do
In fact it was so nice we had to check twice
that it actually came from you!

Thank you very much

Just wanted to say thank you
For what you did for me
I'd love to return the favour
But I don't have the cash you see

Thank You

You've been awfully generous
So here's a big thank you
I can't afford anything more
So this rhyme will have to do

Thank you for a lovely day
You put on a super do
If this is your general standard
Then I'll be over next week too

Sometimes people go out of their way
And their thought makes you ever so happy
Unfortunately the only thanks you'll get
Is this poem, which is rather crappy

You went to such trouble, such a kerfuffle
All that hard work and labour
It was so very nice
That I wouldn't think twice
About returning the favour

There are different kinds of gestures
Some are nice and some cause tension
I've been on the receiving end
Of some too rude to mention

But the gesture that you did for me
Was of the kindest sort
I really can't thank you enough
You are a jolly good sport

Some people don't give a hoot
Don't care if you run or fall
But with your kindness you really do
Put shame to them all

Nothing can express how thankful I am... so that's exactly what I'll give you

I'm unsure how of to say thank you
I could give you a car that's brand new
Or give you my house
Along with my spouse
And all my money in the bank too

Thanks for all that you've done
It's clear you've worked harder than some
Even though it was strained
You never once complained
Or sat around on your bum

You should be recognized
For all you did
That is quite clear to see
You need a cheque
A plaque or a medal
For putting up with me

A thank you
costs nothing...
that's a relief

1st

Seasonal Greetings

Let's raise a glass for St Patrick's Day and toast the Emerald Isle
With our bright green hats and suits, we'll celebrate in style
Once we've riverdanced the night away and sunk a pint or two of beer
We'll wake up with a hangover and do it all again next year

Let's down a pint of the black stuff
And wear a silly green hat
As we celebrate all that's Irish
And the life of old Saint Pat

Strike up the band, bring out the beer
Put on that green suit you made
Let's march through the streets
With a shamrock in hand
And have our own St Patrick's parade

Heavy drinking, wearing green and leprechauns
I can't stand these stereotypes
In fact they bother me so much
I might drink it off in the pub tonight

I'm not environmentally friendly
I don't keep mother earth clean
But on St Patrick's Day
I'm happy to say
I'm more than proud to go green

I don't care for St David
Or that lad St George
Because on their days I've realised
On Guinness I can't gorge

But that good old St Patrick
I'll raise a glass to him
So let's order another
Fill my pint up to the brim

If you find you have nothing to do
And you're just sat at home feeling blue
I'll bring you some cheer
And maybe a beer
And celebrate St Pats with you

When the Irish throw a party
They know how to do it right
So let's make a date to celebrate
This St Patrick's night

I've never been to Ireland and I don't intend to go
But I'll happily toast the Emerald Isle when the Guinness begins to flow

It's a proud day to be Irish
Especially if you are able
To take your fellow Irishmen
And drink them under the table

Apparently it's not funny to scare people out their wits
It's against health and safety to have them rolling round in fits
It's considered quite dangerous to be as gruesome as can be
So I'd appreciate it this Halloween if you'd keep away from me

There are ghostly goings on that are sure to raise a scream
Especially if we visit your house this Halloween
For everybody knows about the creature at your place
The children quake in fear when they look upon his face
Some call it myth some call it legend, some call it orc or elf
But the very scary monster is none other than yourself!

Happy Halloween

I once went trick or treating
I found it a difficult task
But it seemed to work so much better
Once I removed my mask!

There's one thing that's sure to frighten
On this haunted Halloween
Its not ghosts or ghouls or monsters
Just you on too much caffeine

This Halloween we'll throw into the cauldron ...
Eye of newt and toe of frog
Wing of bat and tongue of dog ...
Wait a minute – this sounds like your normal recipe book!

There's a skeleton in the street, there are witches in the air
There's a hairy werewolf that is bound to scare
There's a batch of vampires ready to strike when you're not looking
But the only thing that's scaring me is having to eat your cooking!

Don't come to my house this Halloween, there's a sight you don't want to see
It lives in the darkest corners of my abode, it's always lived with me
It's ridiculously gruesome and hairy, if you stare your eyes will hurt
It isn't a ghost or a werewolf, it's my husband not wearing a shirt!

Last year some trick or treaters
Came knocking at my door
They asked me for some sweeties
But I wasn't really sure
So I said "no, you trick me"
And they did just that
When I got up the next morning
All my car's tyres were flat

Mum and Dad,
I really wanted
to scare you this
Halloween so
I sent you a
copy of our
utility bills

Werewolves appear with each full moon
When the rest of the sky is black
People ask me if I'm a werewolf
I'm not – I just have a hairy back

This year's Halloween
Will be a quiet one I'm sure
I've set up traps in the garden
So the trick or treaters can't get to the door

At Halloween I used to play a good game
Bobbing for apples was its name
I'd like to play now but I'm scared of the grief
In case I should lose my apple and teeth

I get concerned at Halloween; what if I get scared half to death twice!

This Halloween there'll be something ghastly
If in the kitchen you go looking
It wont be the werewolf in the cabinet
But just your scary cooking.

You must love
Halloween...
you dress for
it everyday!

150

I decided to skip Halloween dressing up
It's such a boring task
So I was annoyed and slightly angry
When everyone thought I was wearing a mask

Don't go down in my cellar
There's a dirty secret down there
If you go you'll make a discovery
For which nothing can prepare
It's not a rotting body
Or a zombie resurrection
It's much more frightful than those things
It's my Barry Manilow CD collection

I crept down to the tree last Christmas Eve
To see if the presents were there
And I was greeted by a fat friendly figure
Who was sitting alone in a chair

'Is that you Santa?' I cried out
As it was a convincing disguise
But it was you dressed up in a costume
Stealing my sherry and mince pies!

All I want for
Christmas is you
... and perhaps
a Ferrari.

Christmas is so fantastic that I think we should have it every year.

'Tis the season to be jolly
To feel all bright and perky
'Tis also the season of heartburn
After you've eaten too much turkey

Crackers and turkey, presents and cards
A time of smiles and glee
And when you've eaten your festive fill
You can fall asleep on the settee

Santa said that you were bad and you're on his naughty list
But his strict attention to detail drives me round the twist
So as he's not getting you a present on this Christmas Day
I decided to pop to the shops and get you one anyway

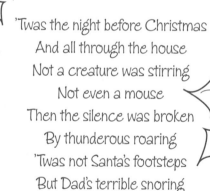

'Twas the night before Christmas
And all through the house
Not a creature was stirring
Not even a mouse
Then the silence was broken
By thunderous roaring
'Twas not Santa's footsteps
But Dad's terrible snoring

In my youth Christmas was spent
Gathered round an open fire
We ate wholesome food and drank malt wine
And of charades we wouldn't tire
But Son, how things have changed
Since those days of turkey and open flames
For you'll spend all Christmas gathered round
The light of your new computer games

If Santa thinks he's got a hard job he should try cooking Christmas dinner for my family.

Why do I buy brussel sprouts each Christmas?
I know they taste like trash
I think next year I'll buy something edible
Or just save myself the cash

Christmas is a magical time
With all the cards stacked on the shelves
Just make sure you're not mistaken
For one of Santa's elves

Happy Christmas

Put the Christmas turkey on
Wrap the presents late at night
And please get someone to lend me a hand
Untangling those fairy lights

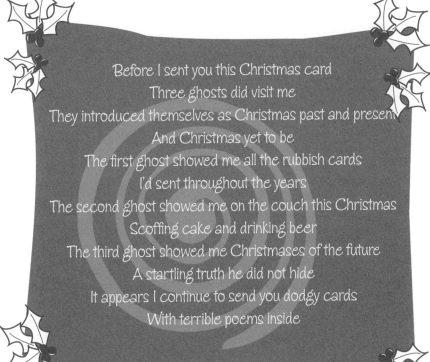

Before I sent you this Christmas card
Three ghosts did visit me
They introduced themselves as Christmas past and present
And Christmas yet to be
The first ghost showed me all the rubbish cards
I'd sent throughout the years
The second ghost showed me on the couch this Christmas
Scoffing cake and drinking beer
The third ghost showed me Christmases of the future
A startling truth he did not hide
It appears I continue to send you dodgy cards
With terrible poems inside

Christmas is fun especially for Dads
Because they love getting socks
And watching the kids ignoring their presents
So they can just play with the box

I hate the Christmas clean up
All the pine needles on the floor
Eating the left over turkey
Taking tinsel down from the door
All the vacuuming takes forever
And that is why I fear
That I'll be doing the Christmas clean up
Until Christmas Day next year

When I was young I would wake my parents
At 5am on Christmas Day
Now I'm old my kids do the same
Although I wish they would just go away

My decorations look so fab
They are the best around
But when I awake each morning
Most of them have fallen down

While wrapping these presents I can't help but think
That the process is such a bore
It will take hours to make them look special
But moments before paper is all over the floor

I'm glad you'll be Christmas present
For our Christmas meal
Or I'd go Christmas crackers
That's just the way I feel

I was thinking of
buying you loads
of presents...
I didn't, but
it's the thought
that counts!

Christmas wishes to you I do send
My family are coming again
They only stay for the day
But if it wasn't that way
Then they'd drive me round the bend

I spent ages writing Christmas cards
With wishes oh so dear
But I wish I could see more of these people
Throughout the rest of the year

When Christmas is white
Everything is all right
We're all so full of cheer
But we'll be really fed up
If our heating packs up
Just like it did last year

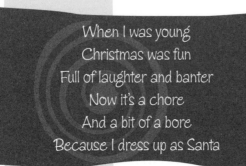

When I was young
Christmas was fun
Full of laughter and banter
Now it's a chore
And a bit of a bore
Because I dress up as Santa

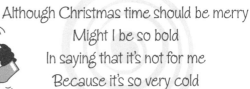

Although Christmas time should be merry
Might I be so bold
In saying that it's not for me
Because it's so very cold

Gather round the Christmas tree
There's no feeling better
And inevitably get the same old gifts
Lots of socks and sweaters

I love Christmas so much
My celebrations have go too far
I have fairy lights all over my house
And hoisted on top of my car

I've got a giant Father Christmas
That I bought in a special deal
I'm just worried what these novelties
Are doing to my electric bill

No wonder Santa is happy
No wonder he's got Christmas cheer
He misses the stress of the yuletide
Only working one day a year

Santa was ill one Christmas
His nose was big and red
He couldn't deliver the presents
So the elves did instead
And after he'd recovered
He was docked a whole years pay
Because lazy Santa Claus
Only works one day

It's important that for Christmas
You don't give pets for presents
Especially if you wrap them up
Without breathing holes or vents

Wishing you a happy Christmas
Full of merriment and cheer
And now I'll make a promise
That I'll see you more next year

We have a Secret Santa
Every year at work
So now I have to buy a present
Instead of trying to shirk

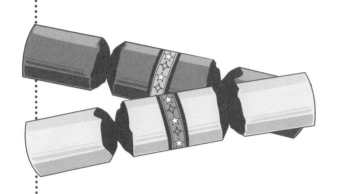

I went out shopping for tinsel
And some wrapping paper too
But Christmas gets me so stressed
That I forgot what I was going to do

When the wrapping and decorating was finished
My mistake was there to see
I'd put tinsel all over the presents
And hung wrapping paper from my Christmas tree

I'm trying to do Christmas on the cheap
Instead of turkey I've stolen a sheep
I'll knock my family out
With cheap wine and stout
So before they're hungry they all fall asleep

There was a huge Christmas present
Under the Christmas tree
And I couldn't believe my luck
When I saw that it was for me

But as I slowly unwrapped
There was just more and more paper
The present was getting smaller
It seemed to be a Christmas caper

And when I finally got to my present
I wanted to complain
Because beneath all that wrapping paper
There was a pair of socks again

When the decorating was finished
Mum said 'put a star' atop the tree
So I placed there a picture of Madonna
Well she's a star isn't she?

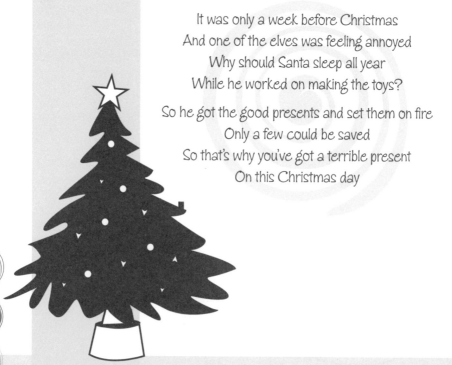

It was only a week before Christmas
And one of the elves was feeling annoyed
Why should Santa sleep all year
While he worked on making the toys?

So he got the good presents and set them on fire
Only a few could be saved
So that's why you've got a terrible present
On this Christmas day

I'll start the day off with a hearty breakfast
Before we get to Christmas dinner
And by the time we get to the pudding
I wont be feeling any thinner
Then when I've scoffed my share of crisps
And stuffing, turkey and greens
It'll only be a drink or two
Before I have to unbutton my jeans

Hope your Christmas is full too!

There are Christmas adverts on TV
Christmas music on the radio
There are Christmas decorations everywhere
And Christmas games in the snow
There are Christmas emails in my inbox
Christmas carollers here to sing
Christmas time is good and all
But you can have too much of a good thing

If you think you've had a rough Christmas ... think what it's like to be a turkey!

Modern day has taken the romance out of Christmas, to me it just seems odd
Children don't want candy sticks, they want a new ipod
It's not good enough to get a toy, they want a brand new gaming console
You can't eat dinner without the 'beep beep' of games, the whole thing's out of control

Before long we'll be gliding to the dinner table on our personal rocket pack
Santa will carry his toys in a manbag instead of hoisting a sack
And we won't send cards for Christmas, we'll send emails to one and all
We'll sit at home surrounded by family via a video conference call

I love a New Year's party
I love Auld Lang Syne
I love to eat the snacks
I love to drink the wine

Every year we have a party
Every New Year's Day's the same
I'll spend the first of January
Clearing up the house again

Every New Year's Eve I make resolutions
Promises that I know that I can't keep
So this year I've made one I'll stick to
That before midnight I'll be fast asleep

Every New Year is a new beginning
A chance to forget the problems and the pain
It's a great night to get groovy, to go and have a boogie
Then make all the same mistakes again

If we were making resolutions
And I had to make one for you
I'd resolve that you do all the chores
Because that way I don't have to

This New Year I promised myself
That I was going to make
A New Year's resolution
To stop scoffing cake

And so I'm on my no cake diet
And I'm sure that you won't knock it
I'm only allowed to eat fruit and veg
As well as biscuits and slabs of chocolate

Keep the Christmas leftovers
Stash all the crisps and beer
Because they always come in handy
When you throw a party for the new year

174

Another New Year is upon us
The time has gone so fast
I just hope that this New Year
Will be better than the last

When all the party poppers are popped
And the champagne has lost its fizz
Then I'll be in no fit state
To tell what year it is

My New Year's resolution is... to complete my New Year's resolutions from last year!

As the clock turns to midnight
And another year passes
I'll be sure to ask for a refill
For all our empty glasses

At New Year I get confused
About the times zones across the land
When 2008 over here
It 2009 in Kazakhstan

Tip
The two years in this verse can be changed

After you've sung Auld Lang Syne
And you've popped your party poppers
Just make sure you celebrate sensibly
Don't get in trouble with the coppers

It's so difficult to send a text to wish you a Happy New Year
The networks are always busy and the lines are not clear
Last New Year's Eve I texted you to hope your time was merry
But the trouble is you didn't receive it until half way through February

Out with the old and in with the new ... out you go then

As New Years go this much I know
My resolutions I'll be keeping
The only promise that I made
Is when it turns New Year's Day
I'll be in my bed and sleeping

Last year I counted the seconds 'til the old year past
I expected fireworks to bang and to blast
But there was no celebration
Across the merry nation
As my clock was running ten minutes fast

I always spare a thought for those working on New Year's Eve
Serving drinks, lighting fireworks, clearing clubs as we leave
And as I climb into bed at 4.15am
I think of all those workers and I'm glad I'm not one of them

For New Year's Eve I give warning
That while the new year is dawning
Don't throw your drink in the air
Without reason or care
Think of who has to clear up in the morning

Cheer Up

Sorry to hear you're under the weather
But surely you're soon to be fine
With all those presents that I've sent you
You'll be back on your feet in no time

For every cloud there's a silver lining
So while you're in pain, coughing and whining
You can settle in bed and raise a smirk
And think of us lot who have to work

Get well soon

I heard about your mishap
You'll soon be on the mend
And before you know it you'll be back at home
Driving us all round the bend

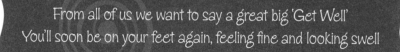

From all of us we want to say a great big 'Get Well'
You'll soon be on your feet again, feeling fine and looking swell

Sometimes you eat something funny
And then you feel less than pristine
You start to get hot and sweaty
And your face begins to turn green
But as you slowly get paler
And you brow gets wetter and wetter
Just know that we all wish you the best
And that you're soon feeling better

182

Although we want to see you better in every kind of way
We realise you've got time off work and you're loving the sick pay

Sorry to hear about your unlucky break
But tell the doctors not to wrap you in plaster
Because although it will help with the healing
You'll also be back to work faster

You may not be very well but at least you'll get better... I'm ugly and that will never change

I know that you don't like hospitals
They leave you in a foul mood
Just try to be nice to the nurses
When they give you hospital food

When you're under the weather and you need to feel better
Then I know the perfect cure
A card like this
Will fill you with bliss
And have you feeling great I'm sure

You're clearly on your last legs
You're as ill as ill can be
So before you pop your clogs
Sign everything over to me

I've been told you are poorly
You look so good I'd never tell
But I hope you make a speedy recovery
And you're soon feeling well

184

I don't know what your problem is
You're obviously not too tough
I'm sure that I've gone into work
When I've been feeling that rough
I don't care what the doctors say
There'll be some facts they're hiding
I know there's nothing wrong with you
Now come on stop your skiving

I know you're in a state because of what was on your plate
Something seems to have disagreed with you
But you'll be feeling fine in next to no time
Ready for dodgy meal number two

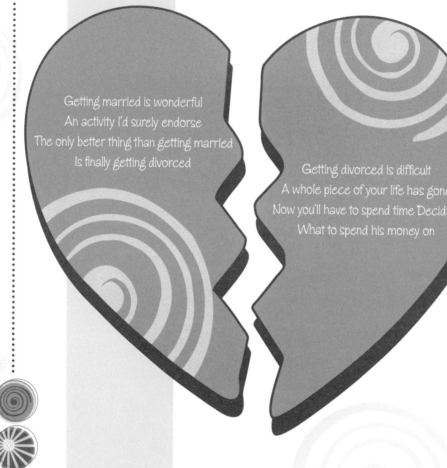

Getting married is wonderful
An activity I'd surely endorse
The only better thing than getting married
Is finally getting divorced

Getting divorced is difficult
A whole piece of your life has gone
Now you'll have to spend time Deciding
What to spend his money on

Divorce is a serious matter
There's no need to mock or laugh
Except when you've gone to your settlement
And walked out with much more than half

There'll be men lining up down the street
Now they've heard about your divorce
And one of them will be your ex
He'll be at your feet in due course

When you next see your ex
Be sure to smile and wink
And then use his cash
To buy something flash
As well as a nice strong drink

Tip
It's easy to change the gender on this one

Suppliers

UK Wholesalers

Crafts Too Ltd
Unit 2 Kingstons Industrial Estate
Eastern Road
Aldershot
Hants GU12 4YA
Tel: (+44) (0)1252 330024
www.crafts-too.com
Wholesaler of craft products importing and distributing ranges from USA & Europe

Design Objectives
www.docrafts.co.uk
Contact them directly through the website or contact Magna Craft on 01730 815555

Personal Impressions
Curzon Road
Chilton Industrial Estate
Sudbury
Suffolk CO10 2XW
Tel: (+44) (0)1787 375241
www.richstamp.co.uk
Visit website or call for your nearest stockists of their craft products from USA & UK. Importers of products listed in USA section

Pergamano UK
Curzon Road
Chilton Industrial Estate
Sudbury
Suffolk CO10 2XW
Tel: (+44) (0)1787 375241
www.richstamp.co.uk
Sole UK importer of Pergamano Parchment Craft Products. Contact for your nearest Pergamano tutor and retailer

UK Retailers

Witzend Arts & Crafts
Witzend
20 Bailey Crescent
Congleton
Cheshire CW12 2EW
www.buycraftsonline.co.uk
Online art and craft retailer specialising in card making – sorry no personal callers. Retailers of products from Personal Impressions and Pergamano UK

Craft Creations
Ingersoll House
Delamare Road
Cheshunt
Hertfordshire
EN8 9HD
Tel: (+44) (0)1992 781900
www.craftcreations.co.uk
Greeting card blanks and general craft retailer. Mail order or contact for stockists

Craftwork Cards Ltd
Unit 2, The Moorings
Waterside Road
Stourton
Leeds
West Yorkshire
LS10 1RW
Tel: 0113 276 5713
www.craftworkcards.com
Sell greetings cards blanks and other specialist card making materials. Mail order available, but visit the shop for the full range of supplies

Fred Aldous Ltd
37 Lever Street
Manchester
M1 1LW
Tel: (+44) (0)161 326 4224
www.fredaldous.co.uk
Originally established in 1886,
this is an Aladdin's Cave of art
and craft materials with craft
workshops available there too

Hobbycraft Stores
Tel: 0800 027 2387
www.hobbycraft.co.uk
General craft retailer
countrywide. Mail order
available or call for your
nearest store

Paper Cellar Ltd
Langley Place
99 Langley Road
Watford
Hertfordshire
WD17 4AU
Tel: 0871 871 3711
www.papercellar.com
Specialize in paper products,
including card making
materials. Buy online or visit
website for nearest stockist

USA

The ranges of craft products
listed here are imported into the
UK by Personal Impressions. See
the UK listing for contact details

American Traditional Designs
442 First NH Turnpike.
Northwood
NH 03261
Tel: 1-800-448-6656
www.americantraditional.com
Embossing stencil manufacturers.
Visit the website for details of
products and local stockists

Artistic Wire Limited
752 North Larch Avenue
Elmhurst
IL 60126
Tel: 630-530-7567
www.artisticwire.com
View a full range of wires and
accessories and locate your
nearest stockist from the website

Art Institute Glitter, Inc.
712 N Balboa Street
Cottonwood
AZ 86326
Tel: 877-909-0805
www.artglitter.com
Projects, products and a gallery
online with details of suppliers
in your area

Magic Mesh
PO Box 8
Lake City
MN 55041
Tel: 651-345-6374
www.magicmesh.com
Full range of products, project
ideas for card making and
scrapbooking, with stockist list

Ranger Industries, Inc.
15 Park Road
Tinton Falls
NJ 07724
Tel: 732-389-3535
www.rangerink.com
Visit website to see vast range of
products for rubber stamping

Suppliers

Tsukineko, Inc.
17640 NE 65th Street
Redmond
WA 98052
Tel: (425) 883-7733
www.tsukineko.com
Manufacturers of unique ink products and craft accessories that fire your imagination

Uchida Of America, Corp.
3535 Del Amo Boulevard
Torrance
CA 90503
Tel: 800-541-5877
www.uchida.com
Manufacturers of art and craft materials for card making, scrapbooking and art projects

USArtQuest, Inc.
7800 Ann Arbor Road
Grass Lake
MI 49240
Tel: 800-766-0728
www.usartquest.com
Visit the website for tips and techniques to help you with your arts and crafts projects

Europe

Kars Creative Wholesale
Industriweg 27
Industrieterrein 'De Heuning'
Postbus 97
4050 EB Ochten
The Netherlands
Tel: (+31) (0) 344 642864
www.kars.nl
Visit website or call for your nearest stockists of Pergamano and other craft products

JEJE Produkt V.O.F.
Verlengde Zuiderloswal 12
1216 BX Hilversum
The Netherlands
Tel: 035 624 6732
www.jejeprodukt.nl
Suppliers of Sandy Art product range, stickers and ahesive products

Pergamano International
Postbus 86
1420 AB Uithoorn
The Netherlands
Tel: (+31) (0) 297 526256
www.pergamano.com
Parchment craft manufacturers. Visit website for product information or nearest stockists

Australia

ParchCraft Australia
PO Box 1026
Elizabeth Vale
South Australia 5112
www.parchcraftaustralia.com
View metal parchment craft tools on website

Canada

Magenta Rubber Stamps
2275 Bombardier Street
Sainte-Julie
Quebec J3E 2J9
Tel: 450-922-5253
www.magentastyle.com

South Africa

Brasch Hobby
10 Loveday Street South
Selby
Johannesburg
South Africa 2001
Tel: +27 11 493 9100
www.brasch.co.za
Manufacturers and distributors of genuine heritage craft products

About the Author
Richard Meade

Richard Meade is from Brentwood, Essex. He has rubbery ears and is fuelled on tea and biscuits. He lives with his wife Jenny and his cat Chipper, who tolerate him with great persistence.

Index

anniversary, wedding 52-61
  1st 59
  10th 60
  30th 61
  20th 61
  couple, to a 55, 56, 57, 58
  husband, to a 53
  parents, to 53
  partner, to a 52, 53, 54,
    55
  wife, to a 52, 57

baby 26-31
  birth 27, 30, 31
  pregnancy 26, 28
best friend 63-69
birthday 9-25
  brother 15
  daughter 12
  teenger 17
  party 125-8
  special ages 11, 12, 14,
    17, 18, 20, 22

china wedding anniversary 6
Christmas 152-71
congratulations 109-117
  driving test 116-17
  graduation 110, 111, 113
  passing tests 109, 110,
    113, 115
  sporting 113

driving test 116-17, 119

engagement 40-45
  couple, to a 42, 44, 45
  woman, to a 45
exams, congratulations
  109, 110, 113, 115

Father Christmas 152, 154,
  155, 162, 164
Father's Day 78-85

good luck 118-123
  driving test 119
  interviews 118
golden wedding anniversary 60
graduation 110, 111, 113

Halloween 144-51
hen party 125
home, new 102-7

invitations 124-31
  bbq 127
  birthday 125, 126
  hen night 125
  housewarming 131
  party 125-8
  stag night 129, 130
  wedding 124

job, new 87-93

leaving home 96

Mother's Day 70-77
moving house 102-7

new home 102-7
  children, to 102, 103
new job 87-93

New Year 172-9

party 125-28
pearl wedding anniversary 61
promotion 88, 89
retirement 100-101
ruby wedding anniversary 59

St Patrick's Day 139-43
Santa Claus 152, 154, 155
  162, 164
stag party 129-30

tin wedding anniversary 60
thank you 132-37

Valentine's Day 33-9
  man, to a 34, 35, 36
  woman, to a 35

wedding 46-51
  anniversary 52-61
  honeymoon 49